The
New Jersey
Reader

By Trinka Hakes Noble
Illustrated by K. L. Darnell

Sleeping Bear Press™

315 E. Eisenhower Parkway, Ste. 200
Ann Arbor, MI 48108
www.sleepingbearpress.com

Printed and bound in the United States.

10 9 8 7 6 5 4 3 2

Library of Congress Cataloging-in-Publication Data

Noble, Trinka Hakes.
The New Jersey reader / written by Trinka Hakes Noble ;
illustrated by K. L. Darnell. —1st ed.
p. cm.
Summary: "This primer is modeled after the McGuffey Readers of the
19th century. Contents include a New Jersey pledge, the Lenape history,
a four season poem, a Molly Pitcher story, a play set during the Civil
War, and a New Jersey timeline"—Provided by publisher.
ISBN 978-1-58536-438-1
1. New Jersey—Literary collections. 2. Readers (Primary)
I.Darnell, Kathryn, ill. II. Title.
PS548.N5N63 2009
810.8'0358749—dc22   2008040747

Preface

New Jersey has always placed great importance on education and learning. The earliest schools were started by the Dutch and Swedish colonists, with records dating back to 1664. The early Quaker settlers believed in education and had schools for all children. New Jersey was the only colony to have two universities. In Bordentown, Clara Barton taught without pay to help successfully establish New Jersey's first free public school. Today over 80% of New Jersey's high school graduates go on to higher learning, the highest in the nation.

The New Jersey Reader is written in the spirit of this long heritage of learning. Patterned after early school primers, it is filled with stories, poems, riddles, nonfiction, drawings, and even a play and timeline, too. I hope you enjoy reading about the state of New Jersey and share this small book with family, friends, and classmates.

Your friend,
Trinka Hakes Noble

For all the wonderful children of New Jersey

T. H. N.

To young artists everywhere, who use their imaginations
to express both what they see and what they hope.

K. L. D.

Table of Contents

A New Jersey Pledge

Once the ancient land of the Lenni-Lenape,
the Revolution's Crossroads became our destiny.

Sitting in the middle, this little colony
forged the link so our country could be free.

With more battles fought for our liberty,
we became our nation's state number three.

Small yet powerful, we pledge our hearts to thee!
This place we call home, the state of New Jersey!

Land of the Lenape

Long ago, New Jersey was part of an ancient land called *Lenapehoking*, which means "Land of the Lenape." For twelve thousand years the Lenape lived peacefully in small villages along its many rivers and streams. *Lenape* means the "common" people. Sometimes they are called the Lenni-Lenape, which loosely translates "We the people." Now they are called the Delaware for the Delaware River which runs through the heart of their ancestral homeland.

The Lenape were divided into several areas. Those north of the Raritan River, including the Delaware Water Gap, were the Munsee, or "people from Minisink, the stony place." Those south of the Raritan were called the Unami, or the "downriver people." Further south, along the Atlantic Coast and Delaware Bay, were the Unalachtigo, or "people near the ocean." The Delaware River connected all three groups.

The Lenape built dugout canoes from the trunks of tulip and elm trees for travel and trade. Some were large enough to carry 20 people and were used in the bays and along the Atlantic Coast. There were also many woodland pathways that crisscrossed the forest floor and connected the villages. Some main trails, like the Minisink Trail, led from the mountains down to the shore where the Lenape would gather each summer to collect clams, oysters, and scallops. Then they made beads and *wampum* from the shells.

Lenape houses were round or oblong, made of sapling poles and covered with bark and woven mats. There was a smoke hole left in the top and the door faced east to greet the rising sun. Everyone worked hard. Men and older boys did the hunting, fishing, and heavy work. Women and children tended gardens, gathered wild berries and nuts, and prepared the food and clothing.

The Lenape were a peaceful nation. When disputes broke out between other East Coast tribes, the Lenape were called in to settle the matter. All Lenape people had a right to speak and each tribe had a wise leader called a *sachem*.

Starting in 1620 Europeans came and settled on Lenape land, often without permission. They brought diseases like measles, smallpox, and mumps, which decimated many Lenape people because they had no natural immunity. Most of the Lenape had disappeared by 1735.

But they left behind many names as a reminder of their long existence. In their language, *Hoboken* means "tobacco pipe," *Absecon* means "place of the white swan," *Watchung* means "hilly place," *Manasquan* means "place to gather grass," and *Allamuchy* means "place of the cocoons."

Yet there are descendants of the Lenape still living in New Jersey today. Just as the Lenape of old, they are determined to pass on their respect and love of the land. We can learn much from their wise council.

Hidden Symbols of New Jersey

State Animal (Horse)
State Insect (Honeybee)
Football (first game played)
State Tree (Red Oak)
Soup Can

State Bird (Goldfinch)
Lightbulb
State Flower (Violet)
Salt Water Taffy
Lighthouse
Beach Umbrella

8

The Garden State

New Jersey is nicknamed the Garden State. The first time New Jersey was called the Garden State was in 1684. A Scottish newspaper printed an advertisement seeking settlers for the new colony of New Jersey. In the ad they called it "the Garden State." The nickname remains to this day and for good reason.

New Jersey is favored with a moderate climate. The winters were not as harsh as New England and the summers were not as hot as the southern colonies. The soil between the Hudson and the Delaware rivers was rich, perfect for farming, especially in the southern

Delaware River region. The Passaic, Raritan, and Hackensack rivers had rich valleys, too. Here, as early as 1630, the Dutch settled and began to farm. They learned how to grow native plants from the local Lenape tribes, and shipped their produce to market on these rivers. Other European settlers soon followed and began to farm.

In 1861 Vineland was created to attract immigrants from Italy who were excellent farmers. Their knowledge and care enriched the sandy

soil to produce many thriving fruit orchards, vineyards, and vegetable farms. Cranberries also thrive in bogs in this southern region. In fact, New Jersey is one of the leading growers of cranberries, which are native to our country.

New Jersey is also a leading producer of blueberries, grapes, freestone peaches, egg-plants, asparagus, pumpkins, tomatoes, and sweet corn. Over 100 different kinds of fruits and vegetables, as well as many fresh flowers, are cultivated here. Many of these well-known varieties were developed at Rutgers University.

Summer and fall are very bountiful seasons with farmers' markets and roadside stands filled with "Jersey Fresh" produce. Even though we are the most densely populated state in the United States, New Jersey can still be called the Garden State.

Four Seasons in the Garden State

Spring

When the violet blooms in **spring**,
then the goldfinch starts to sing.

It's time to plant our Garden State,
with seeds in rows that grow so straight.

Then welcome in the honeybees,
to buzz among our orchard trees.

Summer

Quick, pack the car and shut the door,
we're heading for the Jersey Shore!

We'll stop for tomatoes and fresh sweet corn,
boxes of blueberries picked just that morn.

Then off to the beach for **summer** fun,
and salt water taffy for everyone!

Fall

When the cranberry bogs turn red,
let's head for Jersey's old farmstead.

With bushel baskets, bins, and crates,
full of bounty from our Garden State.

And see all those happy grins,
as we pick our **fall** pumpkins!

Winter

Time to put our garden to bed,
get out the skis, skates, and sled.

Up to North Jersey for some **winter** fun,
our hills and mountains welcome everyone.

Be it winter or spring, summer or fall,
here in New Jersey, we have it all!

The Tale of Tempe Wick

Hidden deep in the old wooded hills of New Jersey is a secluded place called Jockey Hollow. During the winter of 1779-80, the Continental Army camped in Jockey Hollow, hoping its gentle mountains would provide shelter from the bitter cold. But with so many blizzards swooping down, supply wagons could not get through to the 10,000 soldiers.

Conditions were harsh. The soldiers deforested the hills to build log huts and keep warm. They went without food and pay. Many grew sick and dissatisfied. Then it happened. A mutiny started. Desperate times had come to Jockey Hollow.

During this time a young girl named Tempe Wick, short for Temperance, lived in Jockey Hollow. The Continental Army's winter encampment was on her father's farm. Like most New Jersey colonists, the Wicks were patriots. They worked hard and gave what they could. But there was still time for Tempe to do what she loved best, ride her beautiful horse.

Tempe could ride like the wind! Often she was seen flying through Jockey Hollow, galloping to Morristown, speeding over to Mendham, and racing down to Logtown. Because she was such an expert rider, her family often sent her on errands.

It was on one such errand that the tale of Tempe Wick came to be. As Tempe was returning home along a lonely stretch of road, she was suddenly surrounded by mutineers from the Pennsylvania Line.

"We'll be taking your horse, Miss," they demanded as they grabbed her reins.

Although startled and frightened, Tempe was determined not to give her horse to these deserters! With quick thinking, she pretended to dismount.

"To be sure, Sir," she murmured sweetly as she leaned forward.

The soldiers stepped back and let go of the reins. That's when this brave colonial girl dug in her heels and flew away as fast as her horse could run. But they chased after her.

Tempe raced home. She knew the first place the soldiers would look was in the barn so she hid her horse in the house! That's right, this quick-thinking girl led her beloved horse right through the back door, through the kitchen, and around the corner to her little back bedroom, and immediately closed the shutters. Quickly, Tempe ran to fetch water and hay to keep her horse still, then she peeked through the shutters and waited.

Sure enough, those marauding soldiers began snooping around the barn, searching for her horse. Of course, they never thought to search the house! But they kept coming back. Some say Tempe hid her horse in her

bedroom for three days, others say it was three weeks. Eventually the soldiers gave up. Tempe had saved her beloved horse!

Perhaps Tempe was saving her horse for someone special because history tells us she eventually married William Tuttle, a soldier from the New Jersey Line, and lived in the same house where she hid her horse.

You can visit the Wick farm at Jockey Hollow today, and see the little back bedroom where Tempe Wick bravely hid her horse.

Tallyho!

Tallyho and away we go,
to see New Jersey, high and low!

In Elizabethtown we'll start with tea,
and tasty crab cakes for you and me.

On to the Meadowlands for salt marsh hay,
to feed our hungry chestnut and bay.

Over to Morristown's quaint village green,
  we'll watch our soldiers parade so keen.

Then canter on down to Princeton town,
  to study and wear the scholar's gown.

Over to New Brunswick for a pot of stew,
  and a hot biscuit or two would do.

Trot off to Trenton, our capital so fair,
  where Washington crossed the Delaware.

Giddyap, go, and away we fly,
down to Camden for blueberry pie.

Across to Egg Harbor we will ride,
to dig some clams before high tide.

Clippety-clop down to Old Cape May,
and search for diamonds by the bay.

Quick! Gallop fast up the Atlantic Coast,
to outrun those salty pirate ghosts.

Let's build a sand castle without delay,
before the sun sets on Barnegat Bay.

Then on we ride to Sandy Hook,
climb the lighthouse for one last look.

For our two horses do want their stall.
Good night, New Jersey, one and all.

Four "Shore" Fun Riddles

You can find me at the beach.
Kings and queens cannot live in me.
Sand is very important to me.
What am I?

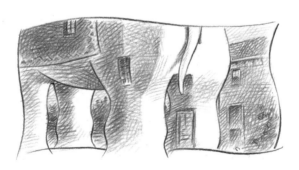

I am gray and six stories high.
People climb up inside me to view the ocean.
I am the largest one of my kind in the world.
What am I?

Dice, money, and luck are important to me.
My streets, hotels, and gardens are named after
Atlantic City.
Kids love to play me.
What am I?

We are called the painted ladies.
We have lots of gingerbread that you can't eat.
Summer visitors love to sit on our porches.
What are we?

The Jersey Devil

So, what's the deal with the Jersey Devil?
Is it myth or real? Is it on the level?

Is it scary and mean? Is it big, bad, and evil?
Has it ever been seen, our New Jersey Devil?

Long ago, in old colonial New Jersey, folks believed in bad omens and evil spirits. They blamed them for a sick cow, a dry well, or a hen that wouldn't lay eggs. No place was this belief stronger than down in the Pine Barrens, that mysterious swampy pine forest that covers much of southern New Jersey.

It was in the Pine Barrens in 1735 that Mrs. Leeds was about to give birth to her 13th child. The story goes that Mrs. Leeds was so tired of having children that she cried out "Let it be the Devil!" At that moment, a cloud of smoke rose up the chimney and the legend of the Jersey Devil was born. 'Tis said it had the head of a horse, wings of a bat, tail of a serpent, hooves of a goat, and the body of a man. For almost 200 years it terrorized the dark and lonely Pine Barrens.

But in 1909 the Jersey Devil was sighted beyond the Pine Barrens. For a week it was seen in towns and cities along the Delaware River, running across backyards and sitting on rooftops. Posses were formed. Curfews were enforced. Children were kept indoors.

Then, in the 1950s, the Jersey Devil was sighted as far north as the Oranges. It was reported that police chased it through the towns. Now, the Jersey Devil can be seen everywhere on posters, T-shirts, and souvenirs, as a symbol of our colorful folklore. We even named our Stanley Cup-winning NHL hockey team the New Jersey Devils after Mrs. Leeds's 13th child, the Jersey Devil.

Crossroads of the Revolution

New Jersey is known as the Crossroads of the American Revolution because it is located in the middle of the 13 colonies, between the Hudson and Delaware rivers. The army that controlled New Jersey could win the war.

The British wanted New Jersey so they could cut the colonies in half. The Continental Army wanted to stop them. So, more battles and skirmishes were fought on Jersey soil than any other colony, over 100 in all.

Between 1776 and 1781 New Jersey became a war-torn land. Its citizens endured great hardship and loss. The armies chased each other across the state four times. The Continental Army camped here for more than half of the war, twice at Jockey Hollow and once at Somerville. Morristown became our country's military capital. General Washington spent nearly a third of the war here, too. He proclaimed it was the efforts of New Jersey that held his army together.

In November of 1776, Washington's army made a hasty retreat across New Jersey to Pennsylvania after being defeated by the British in New York City. It was called the "race through Jersey." Now the British were in control. Things looked bleak. But Washington didn't forget New Jersey.

On Christmas Eve, 1776, Washington made a daring and dangerous move. He ferried his

entire army across the ice-clogged Delaware River to the Jersey side. With cannon wheels and horse hooves muffled with rags, these ragtag soldiers quietly marched through the cold night toward Trenton. Hessians, German soldiers the British hired to fight for them, guarded Trenton. Before dawn the patriots silently set up cannons in the streets and positioned sharpshooters in houses. On Christmas morning when the Hessians awoke, still groggy from their celebrations, the Continental Army launched a surprise attack and took the city back.

This victory lifted the spirits of our new nation. Hundreds of New Jersey patriots joined to fight for independence. Even though New Jersey suffered more than other colonies, this small state played a mighty role in our nation's freedom as the Crossroads of the Revolution.

Molly Pitcher:
A Jersey Girlhood

Mary Ludwig was her real name but history will always remember her as Molly Pitcher. She was born in 1754 on a dairy farm near Trenton.

At an early age Mary was taught to work hard. She had to help with the cows, which means she had to carry buckets of water and milk. Most likely her German father made Mary a small wooden yoke so she could carry two buckets at once. This made Mary a very strong girl.

Mary dressed like most colonial girls but her Dutch mother had her wear wooden shoes to work in the muddy barnyards. Inside Mary went in her stocking feet to keep the house clean.

When Mary was 13 she became a hired girl, which was expected of colonial girls. It was hard for young Mary to leave her home and parents, but luckily she was hired by Dr. and Mrs. Vincent from Pennsylvania. He became a captain in the Continental Army and soon Mary learned the soldier's life.

In time, Mary married an artilleryman and became a camp follower to help her husband and the other soldiers. Often female camp followers were called "Molly" by the soldiers. But it was on her home soil of New Jersey that Mary earned her famous nickname, Molly Pitcher.

On June 28, 1778, the Battle of Monmouth

took place on a very hot day. Washington ordered no cannon could cease firing! In the extreme heat, it was difficult to swab the blazing cannons. Many soldiers collapsed. Mary began carrying pitchers and buckets of water from a nearby spring. Soon soldiers began to call out, "Molly, bring a pitcher please," then "Molly, a pitcher," then finally just "Molly Pitcher."

When her husband was wounded, Mary took his place and kept the cannon firing. After the battle, General Washington made Mary an honorary sergeant, but this brave New Jersey girl will always be known as Molly Pitcher.

John Woolman:
A Jersey Boyhood

Born into a New Jersey Quaker family in 1720, John Woolman grew up on the banks of Rancocas Creek, between Burlington and Mount Holly. John's grandfather was one of the earliest Quaker farmers to settle in South Jersey.

Like all Quaker children, young John went to school where he excelled in writing. His school was a 20-by-20 square log building with few windows. Lenni-Lenape children also attended his school. At an early age, John learned to appreciate all people and respect their ways. Most likely he made friends and played games with the Lenape boys.

An event happened when John was a boy that changed his life forever. One day he threw rocks at a mother robin, just to see if he could hit her. But, unfortunately, he killed the bird. The boy's heart was filled with sadness and regret, especially when he realized she had hatchlings in her nest. Right then, John vowed to love and protect all living things for the rest of his life. He even refused to ride in stagecoaches because he felt it was cruel to the horses. This made John one of the first animal rights activists.

Because John was an accomplished writer, people asked him to draw up important papers. One such document John regretted writing involved the transfer of a slave. Later, he found the woman mentioned in the will and bought her freedom. Native Americans were also held in slavery, too. This went against John's Quaker upbringing. In fact, he only wore white clothing because slave labor was used to produce fabric dyes.

John began traveling about the colonies, speaking out against slavery. As he traveled, he kept a journal, recording everything. Sadly, John died in 1772 but in 1774 his journal was published. *The Journal of John Woolman*, an English literature classic, is the longest continuously published book in North America. It is still in print today.

Thanks to John Woolman, a Quaker boy from New Jersey, the movement to abolish slavery was firmly planted in the American colonies.

New Jersey Firsts

The first log cabin in North America was built in New Jersey by Swedish settlers in 1638. The oldest American log cabin still standing is in Gibbstown, Gloucester County.

Between 1620 and 1650 the Dutch built the first highway, called the Old Mine Road. It was used to haul iron ore from the Delaware Water Gap and still exists today.

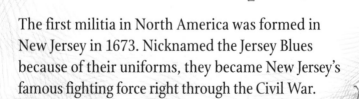

The first militia in North America was formed in New Jersey in 1673. Nicknamed the Jersey Blues because of their uniforms, they became New Jersey's famous fighting force right through the Civil War.

The first continuously operating lighthouse in America was built at Sandy Hook in 1764.

In 1858 the world's first nearly complete dinosaur skeleton was found in Haddonfield and put on public display.

The first intercollegiate football game ever played was between Princeton University and Rutgers University in 1869. One hundred people watched the game.

In 1916 Elizabeth C. White cultivated the first commercial blueberry. Today, all commercial blueberries come from the 11 original bushes she discovered in the Pine Barrens.

New Jersey had the first area code which was 201.

Ely and the Jersey Blues

Chapter One

No Candle for Ely

It was a chilly autumn morning in 1777. As usual, Ely rose before dawn and got dressed in the dark. Ely's father and older brother were weavers by trade. Now that Pa and Daniel were soldiers in the 2nd New Jersey Brigade there was extra work for Ely.

It seemed like everyone was doing something important for the Revolution except Ely. Ma and Priscilla were sewing uniforms day and night. "If Mrs. Washington can knit socks for the soldiers, we weavers can certainly make uniforms," said Ma. Even Grandpa Riggs, with his shaky hands, spent long hours at the loom.

So Ely was left with all the chores and errands. All day he raced about, carrying water, carding wool, chopping wood, delivering cloth, and picking up thread. He had to rise early and dress in the dark because all the household candles were saved for Ma, Priscilla, and Grandpa. They needed good light to sew the uniforms. So there was no candle for Ely.

"Our Jersey Blues deserve our best!" declared Ma. Ely agreed.

But rumors were afoot that the British were scouring New Jersey, searching for traitors. Ma was worried. What if they found the uniforms? But Ma had a plan.

"From now on, we only sew on the tilt-top table," Ma said. "Then, if the British come, we'll flip up the top, hide everything in the little box below, and you children sit on it, by

the fire like a fireside chair. Priscilla, you
spread your skirts over the box and Ely, you
put your leg right over the latch. Then, play
cat's cradle like everything is normal."

Ely and Priscilla thought Ma was very clever.

CHAPTER TWO
Grandpa's Story

That night the wind howled about the house. The family huddled near the fire, listening for any strange sounds outside.

"Grandpa, tell us about the Jersey Blues," pleaded Ely who was trying to get his mind off all the uniforms he and Priscilla were sitting on.

"Yes, please, Grandpa," urged Priscilla who had string ready for cat's cradle, just in case.

"Well, 'twas back in 1673, I think," began Grandpa Riggs slowly, "right here in New Jersey that the first militia in North America was formed. Those early settler soldiers banded together just to protect their settlements and farms. Of course, back then they didn't have any uniforms. They wore whatever they had, their buckskins and fur hats and the like. Your Great-Grandpa Riggs was here then."

Ely liked thinking about those olden times in New Jersey, when the drumbeat of the Lenape echoed through the dark wilderness.

"But they really got the nickname of the Jersey Blues during the French and Indian War."

Ely piped up excitedly, "That's the war you were in, right, Grandpa?"

"Aye, lad," Grandpa smiled. "The story goes that some good New Jersey womenfolk, like your mother and Priscilla, decided our soldiers needed their own uniforms."

Priscilla smiled proudly as Grandpa continued. "So they sewed deep blue breeches and brown homespun jackets for every soldier. Some thought those were the colors of New Jersey, deep blue for the Atlantic Ocean and brown for our good Jersey soil. Since then our soldiers have always been called the Jersey Blues."

"I wish I were in the Jersey Blues," Ely declared.

Suddenly there was a loud *RAP, RAP, RAP* on the door!

Chapter Three
Cat's Cradle

"Open up, in the name of the King!" shouted a gruff voice.

"Children, quick, the cat's cradle!" Then Grandpa Riggs pretended to snooze while Ma calmly opened the door.

"Good evening, Sir," Ma curtsied, using her best manners.

"We'll be searching your house, Madame. King's orders."

"As you can see, Sir, we are but a humble family of weavers. Please, warm thyself by our fire."

The redcoat stomped to the fire. The hilt of his sword flashed in the firelight. To Ely he looked seven feet tall.

"Ah, cat's cradle, I see?"

"Aye, Sir," Ely responded meekly.

"Well, just make sure when the cat's away you little colonial mice don't play!" Then the redcoat poked the tip of his sword into the string cradle and added sternly, "Or you'll be caught in your own game!"

CHAPTER FOUR

Inside Out, Outside In

That night Ely couldn't sleep. He dreamed about big British cats and tiny colonial mice. In the morning, he got dressed as usual in the dark and hurried downstairs.

Grandpa and Ma were talking about the British. "We need a warning system," said Grandpa, "some way to warn our neighbors that the British are snooping around."

"Aye, but how?"

Just then Priscilla laughed. "Oh look, Ely has his waistcoat on inside out!"

Grandpa looked at Ely, and then his eyes lit up.

"Of course!" he exclaimed, snapping his fingers. "I don't know why I didn't think of it before!"

Grandpa took Ely's waistcoat and measured it. Then he began to cut blue cloth and set aside pewter buttons, the special ones with New Jersey written on them.

"Ely, I'm going to make you a Jersey Blue!"

In no time, Grandpa and Ma had made Ely's waistcoat reversible, brown on the outside and blue on the inside. Priscilla expertly sewed double reversible buttonholes so there wasn't a hint of blue on the brown side.

"When the British are around," Grandpa explained, "you wear the plain brown side out and when they are nowhere to be seen, you wear the blue side out with the pewter buttons. We'll spread the word among the people, so everyone will be watching you. You will be the signal. You will give everyone fair warning."

Ely beamed as he tried on his reversible waistcoat. "This makes me a Jersey Blue, brown for our good soil and blue for our Atlantic Ocean!"

Chapter Five
A True Jersey Blue

From then on, Ely was the Jersey Blue signal boy. Folks watched to see which side of his waistcoat was showing. The British were none the wiser. To them, Ely looked like any ordinary colonial boy, doing his chores and running errands.

Then it happened. That spring, at the Battle of Monmouth, Washington's army held fast. The British began to retreat back to New York. Washington ordered the Jersey Blues to tail them, harassing and nipping at their rear guard all the way to the Hudson River.

The British Army retreated through Ely's village, and right behind them marched the

famous Jersey Blues. Ely quickly reversed his
waistcoat to the Jersey Blue side and ran to
march along with them. In no time, he found
his father and Daniel and joined their ranks.
Now Ely was a true Jersey Blue.

Our Noble Friend

Carrying our soldiers, brave and bold,
Pulling the plough in days of old,

Running fast in a steeplechase,
Full of beauty, speed, and grace,

Taking us all for a carriage ride,
Gliding over the countryside,

New Jersey holds you in high esteem,
Home of the U.S. Equestrian Team,

For our state animal is, of course,
Our equine friend, the noble horse!

The Atlantic Flyway

New Jersey is right in the middle of an ancient north-south migration route called the Atlantic Flyway. Because of our location, thousands of birds, waterfowl, and even butterflies depend on New Jersey as a stopover place to rest and refuel as they migrate in the spring and fall.

But at its widest point, New Jersey is less than 60 miles wide. So, to avoid a traffic jam, our geography helps direct these migrating travelers along three main corridors.

The Kittatinny Ridge and Highlands act as a

visual map to help direct traffic. Soaring hawks like the updrafts of this corridor as they migrate to Central and South America.

The next corridor is New Jersey's river valleys. This includes the Delaware and Hudson rivers, plus the Hackensack and Passaic. The Meadowlands and the Great Swamp are welcome stops on this route.

And lastly, the Atlantic Coastal Corridor, from Sandy Hook to Cape May and the Delaware Bay, is one of the most famous in the world. Thousands of shorebirds depend on the many salt marshes, bays, and barrier islands along our 127-mile-long coast.

All three corridors converge on the Cape May Peninsula. This 18-mile-long peninsula is a vital staging place for migrating visitors to safely gather and rest. Here they wait for the right conditions to cross the open waters of Delaware Bay. Thousands of Monarch butterflies feed on Cape May flower gardens before crossing. In fact, Cape May is the best place to witness the Atlantic Flyway, so hundreds of birdwatchers flock there, too.

For the last 350 million years, the world's largest population of horseshoe crabs comes ashore to lay their eggs on the beaches of

Cape May. This ancient ritual coincides with the spring migration of thousands of shorebirds who refuel on the eggs. At this time, these beaches are closed to people.

We must all do our part. Many New Jersey elementary schools have planted butterfly and hummingbird gardens in their schoolyards. Many backyards and town parks are places of refuge, too. As New Jersey was the crossroads in our nation's history, we must also be the crucial crossroads on the Atlantic Flyway for centuries to come.

Thomas Edison:
A New Jersey Genius

Thomas Edison was a longtime resident of New Jersey. Most of his 1,093 different patented inventions were created here. He is considered one of the greatest inventors of all time and was called the Wizard of Menlo Park. In Menlo Park he built a huge research laboratory which was the first of its kind. Most of his inventions are still in use today.

But as a boy, Thomas did not do well in school. His teacher thought he asked too many questions, so his mother homeschooled him. He had a chemistry lab in his basement where he did experiments for hours. At age 12, Thomas went to work selling newspapers on trains. He even wrote and printed his own newspaper which he sold for eight cents each.

When he was 15, he learned to use the telegraph which sent messages in Morse code over electric wires. For the next seven years he traveled all over the United States as a telegraph operator. He improved the telegraph, eventually sending and receiving four messages at once.

But all this time, Edison kept experimenting with other inventions. His first successful invention was a stock market ticker tape that printed both words and numbers which he sold to the Western Union Company. This made him a full-time inventor. He was just 23, but his long life as an inventor had only begun.

Next, in 1877, Edison invented a telephone transmitter which enabled people to hear voices better. Then came the phonograph, or record player. The first words heard were Edison saying "Mary Had a Little Lamb." People were astounded that a voice could be recorded. Edison even made a talking doll that delighted children.

But the greatest invention came in 1879 when Edison invented the first successful electric lightbulb. It burned bright for 40 hours straight. With this invention, Edison changed the world. Now people could have safe, bright light in their homes at the flip of a switch.

In 1889 he invented the kinetoscope which gave us the world's first movie. In 1914 he added sound, and showed a movie on a screen. He thought this would be a wonderful way to educate children in the future.

Edison worked hard on his ideas and inventions, often eating and sleeping in his lab. He never gave up. He believed that anything and everything was possible. Toward the end of his career, he was voted "America's Most Useful Man."

In 1931 Thomas Edison died. He was 84. To honor the passing of this New Jersey genius, everyone in the country turned off their lights for one minute. Even the Statue of Liberty was dark. But Thomas Edison's inventions continue to light up the world every day.

Shoes for Soldiers

Time: The bleak winter of 1864
during the Civil War

Setting: A dingy shoe factory in Newark

Cast of Characters

Mrs. McGreedy: factory owner
Annika: shoe stitcher, age 11
Rachel: shoe stitcher & Annika's little sister
Frankie: shoe cart hauler
Jerome: shoe polisher and packer
Lt. Luke Stockwell: officer in
the 12th New Jersey Infantry
Johnny: drummer boy
Supply officer
Narrator
Sound effects crew

Scene One: The McGreedy Shoe Factory

Narrator: *It is a cold gray dawn on Market Street in Newark. The year is 1864 and the Civil War has been raging for three long years. All the factories in the North are running full steam to supply the Union Army. Many of these factories employ immigrant children who work 12-hour shifts at low pay to help their families. A big order has just come in to the McGreedy Shoe Factory. Massive steam engines roar to life, the starting whistle shrieks, and bedraggled children trudge by Mrs. McGreedy.*

Mrs. McGreedy: (*arms folded, tapping foot impatiently*) Hurry up, you illiterate little donkeys! We've got a big shoe order to fill for the Union Army.

Annika: (*frowns and whispers to Frankie*) I'm not illiterate! I can read and write!

Frankie: (*laughing too loudly*) Ha! If we're all donkeys, then she's an old cow!

Mrs. McGreedy: (*takes hold of Frankie's ear*) Did you say something? I've got my eye on you, Franco Balducci. Watch your step or I'll throw you out. Then all your little brothers and sisters will starve.

Frankie: (*lowers cap over downcast eyes*) Yes, Ma'am... ah...I mean, no, Ma'am. Didn't say nothin'.

Rachel: (*whispers*) Frankie, you're going to get us all in trouble.

Jerome: (*sounding worried*) Don't want no trouble. Can't afford no trouble.

Frankie: (*throws arm around Jerome and Rachel*) Don't worry. I'll watch my mouth. Besides, everybody knows donkeys can't talk!

Rachel and Jerome: (*giggling*) Oh, Frankie! What would we do without you?

Annika: Come on, you three. Let's get to work. Mrs. McGreedy is watching us.

Narrator: *For the next several weeks the children work their fingers to the bone to fill the order while Mrs. McGreedy watches them like a hawk. Frankie collects the shoes from the girls' work station and rushes them to Jerome who polishes, counts, and sorts them by size. Then Frankie hauls large boxes of shoes to the waiting railroad car. As soon as it is full, it will be shipped south to the soldiers.*

Mrs. McGreedy: Work faster, you lazy little donkeys! Lunch will now be shortened to five minutes. I want that railroad car filled by Saturday!

Narrator: *Annika usually read Johnny's letters to everyone at lunch, but the two sisters had not heard from their older brother in months. Now the children are exhausted, growing weaker by the day. Annika is worried. How long can they last? How long will this war last? Can things get any worse? Suddenly, Rachel slumps over her machine.*

Annika: Keep going, Rachel. Old beady-eyes is hiding behind those boxes, watching us. We're almost finished for the day.

Rachel: (*voice trembling*) I don't think I can make it.

Annika: Keep working, little sister, for Johnny's sake. Just a few more minutes before the quitting whistle.

Rachel: I can't, Annika. My fingers won't move.

Annika: (*speaking gently*) Here, I'll help you. Give me the rest of your shoes to finish. We'll make it. Together we'll make it, little sister.

(Stage direction: Stage lights dim and factory sounds fade as the children slowly stop working until they freeze, holding this position until the close of Scene Two.)

Scene Two: A battlefield deep in the heart of Dixie

Narrator: *At that very moment, 500 miles to the south, the 12th New Jersey Infantry is engaged in a fierce battle as artillery shells explode around them. Lt. Luke Stockwell has just given the order for his troops to take cover behind a stone wall. Suddenly there is a loud KA-BOOM! Lt. Stockwell sees Johnny, his drummer boy, stumble and fall. Lt. Stockwell runs back to aid the boy.*

Lt. Stockwell: *(shouting over the battle noise)* Keep going, Johnny! Rebel sharpshooters are hiding behind those trees, eyeballing us. Keep going now. We're almost there.

Johnny: I don't think I can make it, Sir.

Lt. Stockwell: Keep trying, lad. Just a few more feet to that stone wall.

Johnny: I can't, Sir. My feet won't move.

Lt. Stockwell: (*gently removes the boy's shredded shoes and binds his injured feet with his neck scarf*) Here, I'll help you. Quick, put on my shoes. They'll help stop the bleeding.

Johnny: (*flinches with pain*) But, Sir, I can't take an officer's shoes.

Lt. Stockwell: Nonsense! Put them on. Jersey men don't flinch. Together we'll make it, lad! We'll make it!

Narrator: *Lt. Stockwell helps the injured drummer boy to safety. And, at that very moment, 500 miles to the north the quitting whistle blasts through the cold air at the McGreedy Shoe Factory.*

Act Two

Scene One: The next morning
at the McGreedy Shoe Factory

Narrator: *The railroad car is only half full and the children are exhausted. But Annika has a plan. She gathers the children outside the factory entrance.*

Annika: I think we should put a message for the soldiers in all the shoes. Maybe Johnny will find it. Maybe he'll know it's from us. Maybe it will keep him going.

Frankie: (*scratching head*) It's a fine idea but, Annika, it's like putting a message in a bottle and tossin' it in the middle of the Atlantic Ocean. The railroad man told me that 88,000 soldiers are from New Jersey alone. Do you really think Johnny is going to find one of our notes?

Jerome: What if Mrs. McGreedy finds one? What if she reads it? I gotta keep this job,

Annika. You know my mom's real sick.

Annika: I know, Jerome. We all need this job. But *we* need to keep going, too, for Johnny and all our soldiers.

Rachel: (*in small voice*) I know a place we can hide the notes. Let's hide them in the tongue. That's the part I stitch. I'll leave a little opening with a loose thread. No one can resist pulling a loose thread.

Frankie: (*getting excited*) Yeah, and Jerome can slip in the notes before they're boxed.

Annika: (*looking slyly at Frankie*) And, Frankie, we'll need lots of paper and a pencil. Think you can manage that?

Frankie: (*smiling, wiggling his fingers*) Just leave it to me. And, Annika, you do the writing. I don't write so good.

Rachel: Yeah, Annika's the best with words.

Annika: But what shall we say? What should we write?

Narrator: *Just then the starting whistle wails as Mrs. McGreedy stands in the door like an old mule driver.*

Annika: (*whispers to the others*) We'll decide at lunch.

Narrator: *That morning, work didn't seem as hard. Annika was thinking about just the right words. Rachel was testing where to put the little opening with the loose thread. Frankie had paper and a pencil that he'd lifted from Mrs. McGreedy's desk hidden in his pocket. Finally, the noon whistle blew and the children quickly scurried behind a box. They didn't have much time.*

Frankie: (*snickering*) Good thing we don't have much to eat!

Annika: (*smiles*) Right! Now, are we all ready?

Frankie: (*swaggering*) I got the goods!

Rachel: I got the tiny opening figured out.

Jerome: I'm ready and waiting!

Frankie: The train rolls soon so this is it!

Narrator: *Everyone looked at Annika as she carefully wrote words on a little piece of paper. Then she took a deep breath and looked seriously at Frankie, Rachel, and Jerome as they huddled close to listen.*

Annika: These words are for Johnny, our brave soldiers, and us. (*pauses, clears throat*)

We'll keep going if you keep going.
We'll make it if you make it.

Narrator: *For a moment the children were silent, then Frankie nodded and put out his hand. Everyone piled their hands on his and smiled.*

Frankie: (*smirking, head tilted*) Not bad for such dumb little donkeys!

Narrator: *From then on the children tucked as many notes as they could inside shoes for soldiers. On Saturday Frankie ran the last box down to the waiting railroad car. As the train chugged away from the factory, Frankie gave it a farewell salute. All through the night, the Union supply train rolled across New Jersey, picking up shirts from Rutherford, blankets from Passaic, uniforms and firearms from Paterson, cots and tents from Boonton, cannons from Trenton and rain gear from Camden, until it crossed the Delaware River and headed due south.*

Scene Two: Several days later at a Union supply tent in the deep South

Narrator: *The 12th New Jersey Infantry had been pinned down for several days so Lt. Stockwell had to do without shoes. But the army surgeon sent word that the drummer boy's feet were saved, thanks to the lieutenant's quick thinking. Finally, Lt. Stockwell was able to get to the supply tent to get some new shoes.*

Supply Officer: Yes, Sir? What can I do for you?

Lt. Stockwell: I need a pair of shoes, size 12, I think, and a new pair for my drummer boy.

Supply Officer: Just got a new shipment in this morning from New Jersey.

Lt. Stockwell: Did you say Jersey?

Supply Officer: Yes, Sir. Is that your home state, Sir?

Lt. Stockwell: (*wistfully*) Sure is. Wouldn't live anywhere else! If I make it through this war, I am heading back to Jersey.

Narrator: *Lt. Stockwell walked a few feet away from the supply tent, cradling the shoes in his arms, and for a moment, he thought about New Jersey. He thought about its hardworking people and its good land and how much he wanted to be there. That's when he noticed a little loose thread on the tongue of his right shoe. He carefully pulled the thread and a tiny piece of paper fell into his hand.*

Lt. Stockwell: (*speaking to himself*) What's this? (*opens note and slowly reads out loud*)

> We'll keep going if you keep going.
> We'll make it if you make it.

Lt. Stockwell: (*slowly places the small note in his pocket next to his heart, then calls back to supply officer*) Where in Jersey did you say these shoes were made?

Supply Officer: (*checking box*) Newark. The McGreedy Shoe Factory on Market Street.

Final Scene: The McGreedy Shoe Factory, 1865

Narrator: *The Civil War ended in 1865. Lt. Stockwell took the first troop train back to New Jersey. He got off at Penn Station in Newark and walked directly to the McGreedy Shoe Factory. In full dress uniform, he enters the factory holding a pair of shoes. Mrs. McGreedy rushes forward as the factory grows silent.*

Mrs. McGreedy: (*nervous, looking worried*) I see you have a pair of our fine, high quality shoes, Sir. I trust they are to your satisfaction?

Lt. Stockwell: (*holding up a tiny tattered piece of paper*) I found this in my shoes. I would like to meet the person who put it there.

Frankie: (*partially stands, looks nervously at Annika*) There's more than one, Sir.

Annika: (*slowly rising*) I'm Annika. I wrote the words.

Rachel: (*stands and smiles*) I'm Rachel. The loose thread was my idea.

Jerome: (*jumps up with pride*) I'm Jerome. I slipped in the note and gave your shoes an extra shine, Sir.

Frankie: (*standing tall now*) And I'm Frankie. I'm the one who stole the...ah, I mean, I'm the one who made sure your shoes got packed on the train.

Lt. Stockwell: (*stuttering in amazement*) You all did this? But...but...you're just children.

Mrs. McGreedy: (*looking intimidated*) Sir, I had no

idea they tampered with your shoes. I hope it caused you no harm.

Lt. Stockwell: (*looking Mrs. McGreedy straight in the eye*) Madame, I would not be standing here if it weren't for this piece of paper. These remarkable children may well have saved my life! (*turns toward the four standing children*) I salute you four young citizens. You kept me going through the final difficult days of the war. You helped me make it back to New Jersey. For this I will be forever grateful. (*Lt. Stockwell places his hat over his heart and bows*)

Narrator: *In the days and weeks that followed, more grateful soldiers arrived, holding small pieces of paper in their hands. And under Lt. Stockwell's watchful eye, Mrs. McGreedy changed her ways and conditions improved at the McGreedy Shoe Factory. Then, one day, a drummer boy limped into the factory. Four very special children recognized him immediately, and he was given the warmest welcome of all!*

New Jersey Timeline
500 Years of New Jersey History

Lenape Indians inhabit
New Jersey

1500

1609

Henry Hudson explores
New Jersey coast from
Cape May to the Palisades

1620

Dutch settle in
North Jersey

1638
The Swedes settle
in South Jersey

English take over
New Jersey

Newark founded
by Puritans

1664

1666

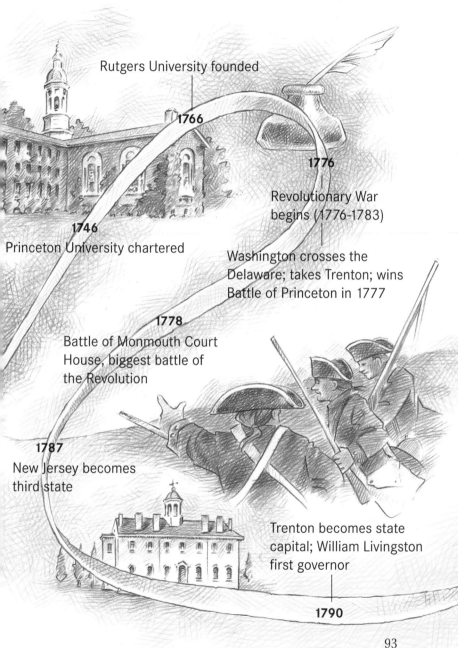

Rutgers University founded

1766

1776

Revolutionary War begins (1776-1783)

1746
Princeton University chartered

Washington crosses the Delaware; takes Trenton; wins Battle of Princeton in 1777

1778
Battle of Monmouth Court House, biggest battle of the Revolution

1787
New Jersey becomes third state

Trenton becomes state capital; William Livingston first governor

1790

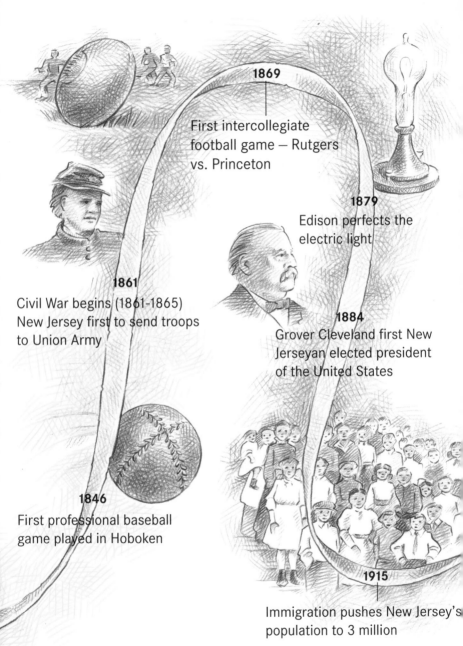

1869
First intercollegiate football game – Rutgers vs. Princeton

1879
Edison perfects the electric light

1861
Civil War begins (1861-1865) New Jersey first to send troops to Union Army

1884
Grover Cleveland first New Jerseyan elected president of the United States

1846
First professional baseball game played in Hoboken

1915
Immigration pushes New Jersey's population to 3 million

94

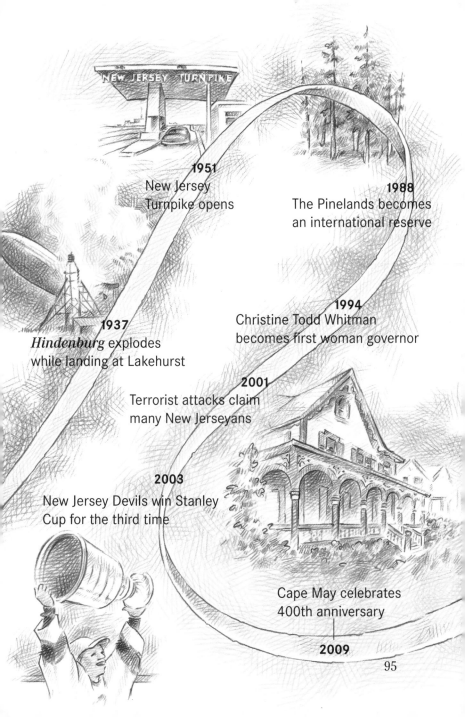

1951
New Jersey
Turnpike opens

1988
The Pinelands becomes
an international reserve

1994
Christine Todd Whitman
becomes first woman governor

1937
Hindenburg explodes
while landing at Lakehurst

2001
Terrorist attacks claim
many New Jerseyans

2003
New Jersey Devils win Stanley
Cup for the third time

Cape May celebrates
400th anniversary

2009

95

The Little Giant

From our Highland mountains with wooded glens,
To the sandy wetlands of the Pine Barrens,

With the Atlantic Ocean standing by our side,
We are a little giant full of power and pride.

For it is our many people that make us so strong,
Even though we're only 160 miles long.

So New Jersey is a giant, though small in size,
Packed with success and power, a state to prize!

Trinka Hakes Noble

Trinka Hakes Noble is the award-winning author of numerous picture books including *The Scarlet Stockings Spy* (an IRA Teachers' Choice 2005), *The Last Brother*, and *The Legend of the Cape May Diamond*. Ms. Noble also wrote the ever-popular *Jimmy's Boa* series and *Meanwhile Back at the Ranch*, both featured on PBS's *Reading Rainbow*. Her many awards include ALA Notable Children's Book, *Booklist* Children's Editors' Choice, IRA-CBC Children's Choice, *Learning*: The Year's Ten Best, and several Junior Literary Guild selections.

Ms. Noble has studied children's book writing and illustrating in New York City at Parsons School of Design, the New School University, Caldecott medalist Uri Shulevitz's Greenwich Village Workshop, and at New York University. A member of the Rutgers University Council on Children's Literature, she was awarded Outstanding Woman 2002 in Arts and Letters in the state of New Jersey for her lifetime work in children's books. Ms. Noble lives in northern New Jersey. Learn more at www.trinkahakesnoble.com.

K. L. Darnell

K. L. Darnell has been drawing pictures for as long as she can remember. She earned her BFA studying drawing and painting at the University of Michigan School of Art and Design. *The New Jersey Reader* is Ms. Darnell's tenth children's book with Sleeping Bear Press. In addition to her work as an illustrator, she specializes in the beautiful art of calligraphy and is an instructor of art at Lansing Community College. Ms. Darnell lives and works in East Lansing, Michigan.